MAY 2 4 1999

DEC 1 1 1998   JUN 1 3 2003   NOV 2 0 2000

NOV 1 1999

JAN 0 4 1999   SEP 2 3 1999

JAN 1 0 1999   OCT 2 0 1999

APR 0 1 2003   NOV 0 9 1999

JAN 2 OCT 0 6 2002

NOV 3 0 1999

DEC 0 1 2003   FEB. 1 4 2000

OCT   6 2005   OCT 0 9 2014

FEB 1 7 2000

DEC 2 1 2015

NOV 1 7 2017

DEMCO

HARLEY-DAVIDSON

HARLEY-DAVIDSON

HUGO WILSON

DORLING KINDERSLEY

DK PUBLISHING, INC.

A DK PUBLISHING BOOK

PROJECT EDITOR PHIL HUNT
ART EDITOR MARK JOHNSON DAVIES

SENIOR EDITOR LOUISE CANDLISH
SENIOR ART EDITOR HEATHER McCARRY
MANAGING EDITOR ANNA KRUGER
DEPUTY ART DIRECTOR TINA VAUGHAN
US EDITOR RAY ROGERS
PRODUCTION CONTROLLER ALISON JONES

First American edition, 1998

2 4 6 8 10 9 7 5 3 1

Published in the United States by DK Publishing, Inc.,
95 Madison Avenue, New York, New York 10016

Visit us on the World Wide Web at http://www.dk.com

Library of Congress Cataloging-in-Publication Data

Wilson, Hugo
  Harley-Davidson / by Hugo Wilson. -- 1st American ed.
    p.   cm. -- (Classic motorcycles)
  ISBN 0-7894-3506-3
  1. Harley-Davidson motorcycle--History.   I. Title   II. Series.
TL448.H3W56   1998
629.227'5--dc21
                                                             98-17162
                                                                  CIP

Harley-Davidson is a registered trademark of Harley-Davidson Limited.

Reproduced by Colourscan, Singapore
Printed in Hong Kong

CONTENTS

INTRODUCTION

Think of America and you think of
the Statue of Liberty, the Golden
Gate Bridge, James Dean, Elvis
Presley, Coca-Cola, blue jeans, and
Harley-Davidson motorcycles. The
metal, chrome, bold paint, and
throbbing sound of the classic
Harley has become an international
symbol of the American dream.
When you consider the story of a
group of friends who built a
motorcycle in a backyard shed
and created the most famous
motorcycle marque in the world,
it encompasses the American ideal
of dreams becoming reality. The
appeal of a Harley is more about
romance than it is about metal.

HUGO WILSON

HARLEY-DAVIDSON TIMELINE

IT IS NEARLY 100 YEARS SINCE the first Harley-Davidson motorcycle was built in a shed in Milwaukee, Wisconsin, and today's bikes have a direct line of descent from that first machine. Harley's conservative management never rushed into change, and it has paid dividends. Now Harley makes full use of its heritage and produces bikes that take their styling cues from earlier machines. In silhouette, it would be hard to differentiate a 1935 bike from one built 60 years later.

SILENT GRAY
FELLOW

THE EARLY DAYS

The outline of this 1912 Silent Gray Fellow shows the obvious relationship between the bicycle and early motorcycle design. The single-speed machine needs pedals to start and to help it climb hills.

• 1910s •	• 1920s	• 1930s	• 1940s	• 1950

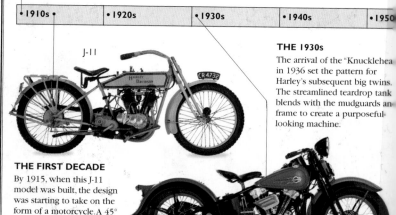

J-11

THE 1930s

The arrival of the "Knucklehea[d]" in 1936 set the pattern for Harley's subsequent big twins. The streamlined teardrop tank blends with the mudguards an[d] frame to create a purposeful-looking machine.

THE FIRST DECADE

By 1915, when this J-11 model was built, the design was starting to take on the form of a motorcycle. A 45° V-twin engine was fitted into a longer, lower frame, and a three-speed gearbox came as standard.

KNUCKLEHEAD

SIDE-VALVE STRATEGY

Harley began developing side-valve engines in the 1920s as its inlet-over-exhaust valve layouts became dated. The overhead-valve "Knucklehead" engine appeared in 1936, but Harley stuck with the side-valve for its smaller V-twins until 1957. Even then, racers like this K Series bike retained the side-valve engine until the late 1960s.

Cylinder barrel also contains inlet and exhaust ports

KR750

• 1960s • 1970s • 1980s • 1990s

DUO GLIDE

ROAD KING

THE 1960s

The stylish Duo Glide earned Harley-Davidson much respect. It was the perfect long-distance tourer, and its classic design provided the blueprint for subsequent models.

THE 1990S AND BEYOND

Harley-Davidson will apply technological advances only if they are in harmony with its traditional values, as this 1997 Road King demonstrates.

1912 SILENT GRAY FELLOW

• THE FIRST HARLEY •

HARLEY-DAVIDSON GAINED A REPUTATION early on for practicality and dependability, based partly on the power of its engines and the strength of its frames. Harleys were among the first truly practical motorcycles on the market. By the time this bike was built in 1912, the basic design had been upgraded – engine capacity had increased to 30cu. in., and a sprung front fork was fitted. The following year, the automatic inlet valve was finally dropped. The rugged dependability of the bike gave rise to its name, "The Silent Gray Fellow."

White rubber tires were a period feature

Sprung fork

Leading-link front suspension

Schebler carburetor

SIDE VIEW

SPECIFICATIONS

- **ENGINE** Inlet-over-exhaust, single cylinder
- **CAPACITY** 30cu. in. (494cc)
- **POWER OUTPUT** 6.5bhp @ 2,700rpm
- **TRANSMISSION** Single speed, belt drive
- **WEIGHT** 195lb (88.5kg)
- **TOP SPEED** 45mph (72km/h)

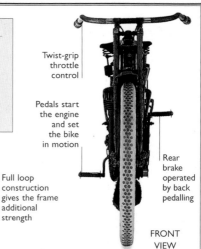

Twist-grip throttle control

Pedals start the engine and set the bike in motion

Rear brake operated by back pedalling

FRONT VIEW

Lever controls clutch in rear wheel hub

Full loop construction gives the frame additional strength

Battery box for coil ignition

Belt tensioning pulley

Rear stand

1915 J-11

• ONE OF HARLEY'S EARLIEST V-TWINS •

THE V-TWIN ENGINE LAYOUT ALLOWED early manufacturers to increase power outputs with minimal tooling or development costs. A new crankshaft and engine cases allowed two cylinders to be fitted in a "V" formation, producing twice the power of a single-cylinder machine. When Harley made its first V-twin in 1907, it chose the 45° cylinder arrangement that it still uses today. By 1915, the design had developed into the model shown here, with a three-speed gearbox, all-chain drive, a foot-operated clutch, and a mechanical oil pump.

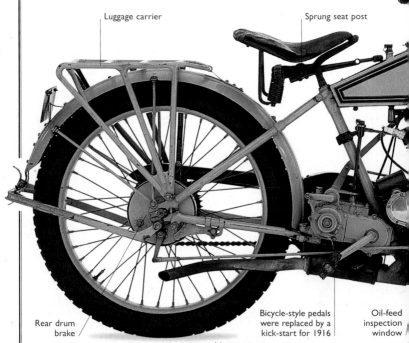

Luggage carrier

Sprung seat post

Rear drum brake

Bicycle-style pedals were replaced by a kick-start for 1916

Oil-feed inspection window

FOUNDING BROTHERS

The first Harley-Davidson was built in 1903 by William S. Harley and his friend Arthur Davidson. Arthur's brothers, William and Walter Senior, soon joined the project. Members of the Davidson family are still involved in the business today.

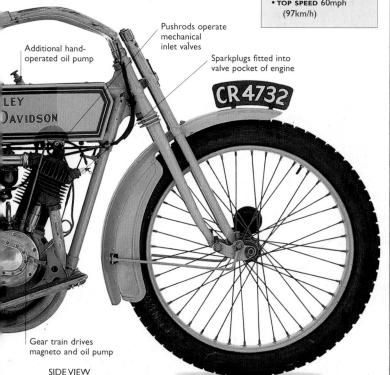

Pushrods operate mechanical inlet valves

Additional hand-operated oil pump

Sparkplugs fitted into valve pocket of engine

CR 4732

HARLEY DAVIDSON

Gear train drives magneto and oil pump

SIDE VIEW

1926 B PEASHOOTER

• SUCCESS WITH A SINGLE CYLINDER •

CHEAP, UTILITARIAN MOTORCYCLES SOLD WELL in domestic and export markets in the 1920s. Harley-Davidson introduced a 21cu. in. single-cylinder machine in 1926 that was available with side-valve or overhead-valve engines and with or without lights. The bike was similar in style to British machines and to the contemporary American-built Indian Prince. Although it sold in reasonable numbers both at home and abroad and competition versions found success in speedway racing, production ended in 1929. The "Peashooter" nickname derived from the bike's distinctive exhaust note.

Olive green paint was Harley's standard finish of the period

Bicycle-style seat

Side-valve cylinder head designed by Harry Ricardo

Tool roll

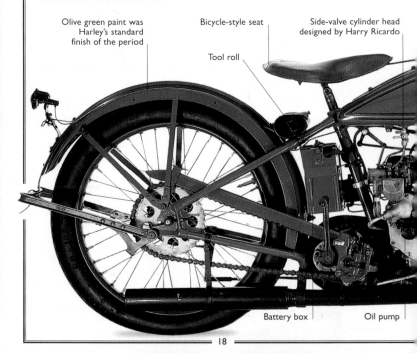

Battery box

Oil pump

SPECIFICATIONS

- **ENGINE** Side-valve, single cylinder
- **CAPACITY** 21cu. in. (346cc)
- **POWER OUTPUT** 10bhp
- **TRANSMISSION** Three-speed, chain drive
- **WEIGHT** 263lb (119kg)
- **TOP SPEED** 60mph (96.5km/h)

Klaxon

Gear lever

FRONT VIEW

Instrument panel

Exposed springs

"Clincher" wheel rim

Suspension linkage

SIDE VIEW

Front wheel without brake

1936 61EL KNUCKLEHEAD

• GRANDFATHER OF THE BIG TWINS •

THE "KNUCKLEHEAD" WAS ONE OF HARLEY'S most important models. Its combination of good looks, excellent performance, and mechanical innovation helped Harley overtake Indian as America's prime motorcycle producer. The grandfather of the current range of big twins, it was Harley's first V-twin road bike with overhead valves, a recirculating lubrication system, and positive-stop four-speed gearbox, and it was produced in low- and high-compression versions. The featured bike is a rare high-compression EL model, but an even sportier 74cu. in. block was introduced in 1941. The "Knucklehead" nickname arises from the appearance of the pushrod tubes and rocker pivots.

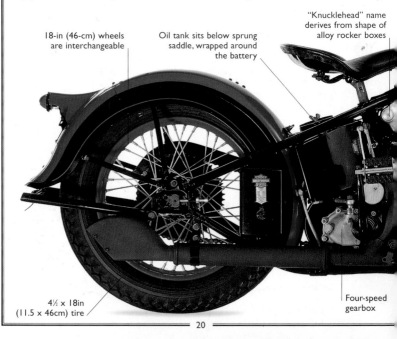

"Knucklehead" name derives from shape of alloy rocker boxes

18-in (46-cm) wheels are interchangeable

Oil tank sits below sprung saddle, wrapped around the battery

4½ x 18in (11.5 x 46cm) tire

Four-speed gearbox

SPECIFICATIONS

- **ENGINE** Overhead-valve, V-twin
- **CAPACITY** 61cu. in. (988cc)
- **POWER OUTPUT** 40bhp @ 4,800rpm
- **TRANSMISSION** Four-speed, chain drive
- **WEIGHT** 515lb (234kg)
- **TOP SPEED** 100mph (161km/h)

Crash bars

Chrome horn cover

Kick-start

FRONT VIEW

Two-part fuel tank houses instrument panel

Horn

Friction suspension damper

Air filter

SIDE VIEW

1942 WLA

• WARTIME WORKHORSE •

HARLEY FIRST INTRODUCED A 45CU. IN. side-valve V-twin in 1929 in response to the very successful Indian Scout. Eight years later, the same engine configuration was used in the new W Series and provided the basis of Harley's wartime output for the Allied military forces. Over 80,000 WLA and WLC machines were produced during World War II, and it was only with the widespread introduction of the Willy's Jeep that output declined. Military-spec WLA models were devoid of all unnecessary trim and featured upgraded air filters, bashplates, and mudguards, as well as the obvious military modifications such as gun holsters and blackout lighting. Harley continued to build 45cu. in. side-valves for the civilian market until 1955, but its racers and the Servi-car tricycle used these engines long after this date.

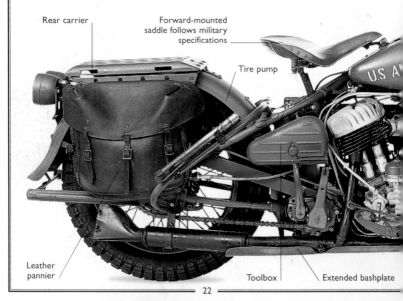

Rear carrier

Forward-mounted saddle follows military specifications

Tire pump

U.S A

Leather pannier

Toolbox

Extended bashplate

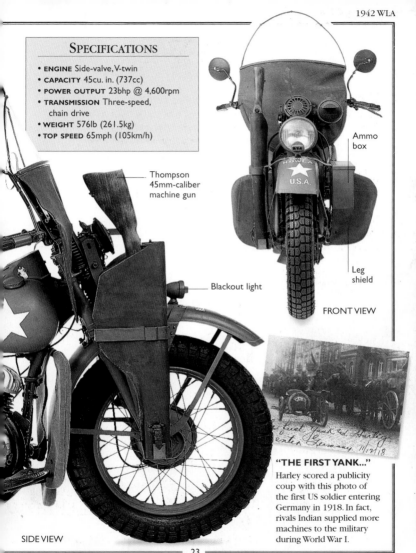

SPECIFICATIONS

- **ENGINE** Side-valve, V-twin
- **CAPACITY** 45cu. in. (737cc)
- **POWER OUTPUT** 23bhp @ 4,600rpm
- **TRANSMISSION** Three-speed, chain drive
- **WEIGHT** 576lb (261.5kg)
- **TOP SPEED** 65mph (105km/h)

Ammo box

Thompson 45mm-caliber machine gun

Leg shield

Blackout light

FRONT VIEW

"THE FIRST YANK..."
Harley scored a publicity coup with this photo of the first US soldier entering Germany in 1918. In fact, rivals Indian supplied more machines to the military during World War I.

SIDE VIEW

1951 74FL

• MORE IMPROVEMENTS TO THE BIG TWIN •

Two critical improvements were undertaken on Harley's big twins as the 1950s approached. The famous "Knucklehead" engine was redesigned for 1948 with the valvegear totally enclosed under large rocker covers. The appearance of these covers was accurately described in the nickname given to the new engine – "Panhead." The second development came a year later when hydraulically damped telescopic forks were introduced and, to celebrate this improvement in comfort, the "Hydra-Glide" model name was introduced. In Harley's lettering system, F signifies 74cu. in. engine and L is high compression. Harley's big twins were always a popular choice for police work, especially after the demise of Indian in 1953 removed any domestic competition.

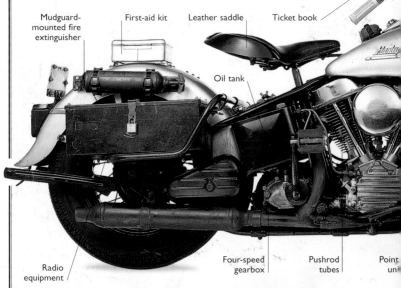

Mudguard-mounted fire extinguisher

First-aid kit

Leather saddle

Ticket book

Oil tank

Four-speed gearbox

Pushrod tubes

Point uni

Radio equipment

SPECIFICATIONS

- **ENGINE** Overhead-valve, V-twin
- **CAPACITY** 74cu. in. (1213cc)
- **POWER OUTPUT** 55bhp
- **TRANSMISSION** Four-speed, chain drive
- **WEIGHT** 598lb (271kg)
- **TOP SPEED** 102mph (164km/h)

Red pursuit light

Mudguard-mounted police sign

A RELIABLE COMPANION

This 1951 Harley was used by the Police Department of Willowick, Ohio, for 36 years. During that time it got little use but plenty of attention. While the police preferred patrol cars, their mechanics loved motorcycles.

Crash bar

SIDE VIEW

SALES LITERATURE

Police sales were potentially profitable, and Harley eagerly sought them with special promotional campaigns.

1952 52K

• A STYLISH RESPONSE TO FOREIGN COMPETITION •

Large numbers of British machines began arriving in America in the early 1950s. The imports were lighter, faster, and handled better than the domestic product. Harley responded by introducing a new 45cu. in. side-valve machine in 1952. The K had front and rear suspension and a new unit-construction engine featuring a right-foot shift gearbox. It looked good, too, but it wasn't fast enough to stay with British-built 500cc and 650cc overhead-valve parallel twins. Even increasing capacity to 54cu. in. to create the KH in 1954 was not enough to convince potential buyers.

Horn

Drum brake

SIDE VIEW

SPECIFICATIONS

- **ENGINE** Side-valve, V-twin
- **CAPACITY** 45cu. in. (737cc)
- **POWER OUTPUT** 30bhp (est.)
- **TRANSMISSION** Four-speed,
  chain drive
- **WEIGHT** 400lb (181kg)
- **TOP SPEED** 85mph (136km/h) (est.)

"Cow horn" handlebars

Telescopic forks with chrome shrouds

Crash bar

Uprated 4½-gallon (20.5-liter) fuel tank

19-in (48-cm) wheels higher and narrower than on previous models

FRONT VIEW

Enclosed primary drive case – the four-speed gearbox was built in unit with engine

Swingarm rear suspension

1957 XL SPORTSTER

• A CLASSIC IS BORN •

FROM THE COMPARATIVE FAILURE OF THE K SERIES, Harley's longest-surviving model was developed. The XL Sportster was introduced in 1957 and, updated and improved but maintaining the same style, remains an essential part of Harley's range today. The side-valve breathing system of the K Series engine was replaced with a more modern overhead-valve arrangement, and the bore and stroke of the crankshaft were upgraded. This increased power sufficiently to put the Sportster on an equal performance footing with the British-built opposition.

Optional luggage rack and panniers

Optional crash bars fitted front and rear

Iron cylinder head and barrel; alloy heads weren't fitted until the 1980s

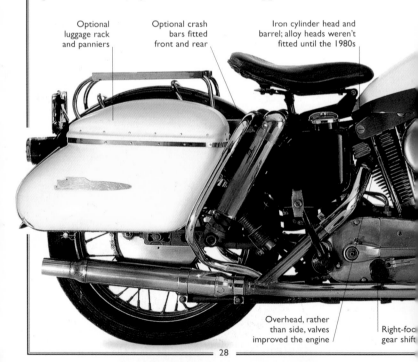

Overhead, rather than side, valves improved the engine

Right-foo gear shift

Windshield

SPECIFICATIONS

- **ENGINE** Overhead-valve, V-twin
- **CAPACITY** 54cu. in. (883cc)
- **POWER OUTPUT** 32bhp @ 4,200rpm
- **TRANSMISSION** Four-speed, chain drive
- **WEIGHT** 463lb (210kg)
- **TOP SPEED** 92mph (148km/h) (est.)

Frame and cycle parts taken from earlier K Series

Chrome fork slider

FRONT VIEW

Redesigned fuel tank, livery, and logo

SIDE VIEW

Single leading-shoe drum brake

1960 FLH DUO GLIDE

• AMERICA'S DEFINITIVE TOURING BIKE •

FITTING REAR SUSPENSION TO THE 74CU. IN. Panheads in 1958 justified the new "Duo Glide" model name. The increased comfort confirmed Harley's big twin as the definitive touring machine for American roads, where its low-revving V-twin engine was capable of covering long distances. To increase its practicality as a tourer, most owners specified screens, panniers, and other touring accessories, so these fully equipped machines were known as "dressers." When an electric starter was offered in 1965, the famous Electra Glide was born.

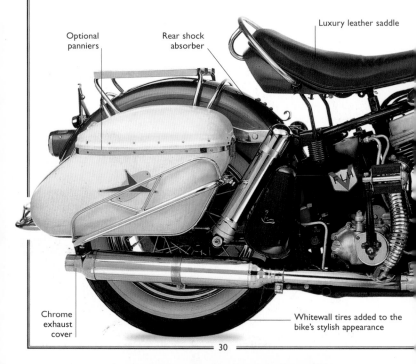

Optional panniers

Rear shock absorber

Luxury leather saddle

Chrome exhaust cover

Whitewall tires added to the bike's stylish appearance

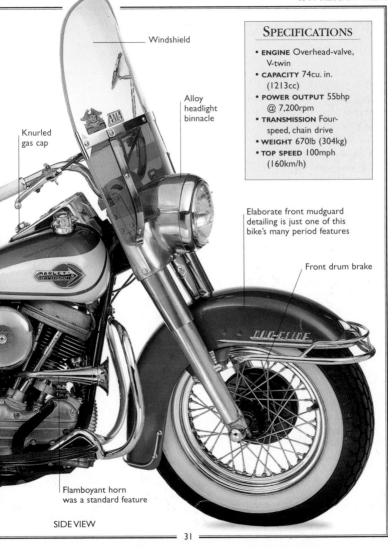

Windshield

Alloy
headlight
binnacle

Knurled
gas cap

SPECIFICATIONS

- **ENGINE** Overhead-valve,
  V-twin
- **CAPACITY** 74cu. in.
  (1213cc)
- **POWER OUTPUT** 55bhp
  @ 7,200rpm
- **TRANSMISSION** Four-
  speed, chain drive
- **WEIGHT** 670lb (304kg)
- **TOP SPEED** 100mph
  (160km/h)

Elaborate front mudguard
detailing is just one of this
bike's many period features

Front drum brake

HARLEY-DAVIDSON

DUO-GLIDE

Flamboyant horn
was a standard feature

SIDE VIEW

31

1961 KR750

• A WINNING PACKAGE •

THE BIZARRE REGULATIONS UNDER WHICH American motorcycle racing was run in the 1950s and '60s kept side-valve Harleys in the winner's circle long after they had passed their sell-by date as road bikes. They may have been archaic, but the side-valve KR racers were handsome and highly effective machines. This bike won the 1961 Daytona 200-mile road race in the hands of Harley racing legend Roger Reiman. For this event, which was run on Daytona's famous banked oval track, the bike was fitted with a larger fuel tank and brakes.

WINNING HARLEY
This is Roger Reiman's winner's flag from the 1961 Daytona 200 race.

Clip-on handleb
used on long
straights to
reduce drag

Alloy
wheel
rim

FRONT VIEW

SIDE VIEW

SPECIFICATIONS

- **ENGINE** Side-valve, V-twin
- **CAPACITY** 45cu. in. (750cc)
- **POWER OUTPUT** 50bhp
- **TRANSMISSION** Four-speed, chain drive
- **WEIGHT** 320lb (145kg)
- **TOP SPEED** 125mph (233km/h)

RACE PEDIGREE

The Daytona 200 was one of many racing trophies won by Harley. It debuted in motorcycle racing back in 1909.

Wide bars for dirt-track use

Large fuel tank for long-distance races

Traditional Harley side-valve engine

Brake pedal has been drilled to reduce weight

1965 BOBCAT

• THE LAST AMERICAN LIGHTWEIGHT •

HARLEY ACQUIRED THE RIGHTS TO BUILD a small-capacity two-stroke engine from the German firm DKW as part of reparations after World War II. It built bikes based on this engine from 1947 until 1966. The Bobcat, with its unusual fiberglass seat/tank unit, was a rather forlorn attempt to compete with the new breed of Japanese lightweight machines that were selling in large numbers in the US at the time. Harley bought a big slice of the Italian Aermacchi factory in 1960, and from 1966 all of Harley's lightweights were made in Italy.

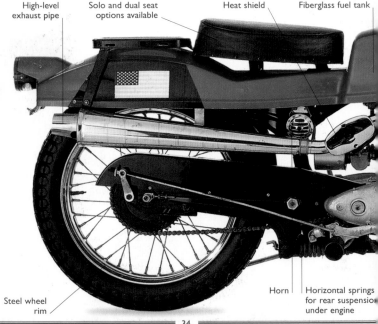

High-level
exhaust pipe

Solo and dual seat
options available

Heat shield

Fiberglass fuel tank

Horn

Horizontal springs
for rear suspension
under engine

Steel wheel
rim

Wing mirror

Speedometer

Specifications

- **ENGINE** Single cylinder, two-stroke
- **CAPACITY** 175cc
- **POWER OUTPUT** 10bhp (est.)
- **TRANSMISSION** Three-speed, chain drive
- **WEIGHT** Not known
- **TOP SPEED** 65mph (105km/h) (est.)

Short-travel front suspension

Gaiter for telescopic fork

FRONT VIEW

Steel mudguard

Single downtube frame

Narrow front drum brake

SIDE VIEW

1972 XRTT

• OFF THE DIRT AND INTO THE TRACK •

HARLEY V-TWINS HAVE ALWAYS BEEN effective in American dirt-track racing, but they have only occasionally been used in road racing. The letters "TT" indicate that this bike is a rare road-racing version of the 1972 XR dirt-track machine. Changes from the dirt-track bike include the omission of air filters and the addition of appropriate bodywork and brakes. The engine is all-alloy with forward-facing exhaust ports and rear-facing inlet ports fed by twin Mikuni carburetors. The legendary Cal Rayborn used this bike successfully during the 1972 season.

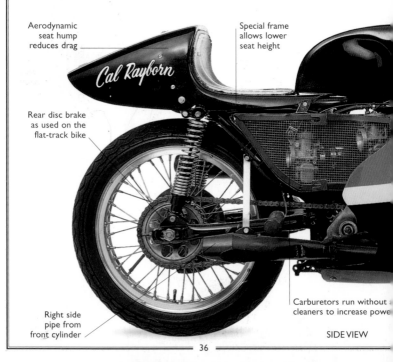

Aerodynamic seat hump reduces drag

Special frame allows lower seat height

Rear disc brake as used on the flat-track bike

Right side pipe from front cylinder

Carburetors run without air cleaners to increase power

SIDE VIEW

SPECIFICATIONS

- **ENGINE** Overhead-valve, V-twin
- **CAPACITY** 45cu. in. (750cc)
- **POWER OUTPUT** 90bhp @ 8,000rpm
- **TRANSMISSION** Four-speed,
  chain drive
- **WEIGHT** 324lb (147kg)
- **TOP SPEED** 130mph (209km/h) (est.)

Sculpted 6-
gallon (23-
liter) fuel tank
allows rider
to "tuck in"

Exhaust
from rear
cylinder

Period
Harley-
Davidson
race logo

Front
cylinder
exhaust
pipe

BACK VIEW

Alloy
wheel
rim

Fairing painted in
Harley-Davidson
racing colors

Ceriani four
leading-shoe
drum brake

1987 XLH883 SPORTSTER

• A HARLEY FOR A NEW GENERATION •

FROM 1969 TO 1981 HARLEY-DAVIDSON was owned by AMF, and during that time the reliability, performance, and quality of the bikes suffered. Following the management buyout in 1991, the bikes were reengineered – while maintaining the traditional style of the machines – and quality control was improved. The 883 Sportster was introduced in 1986 as a fun and affordable machine that would attract new buyers to the marque. The new all-alloy engine unit was quieter and more reliable than earlier Sportsters and gave Harley's new customers the classic Harley image without the usual technical problems.

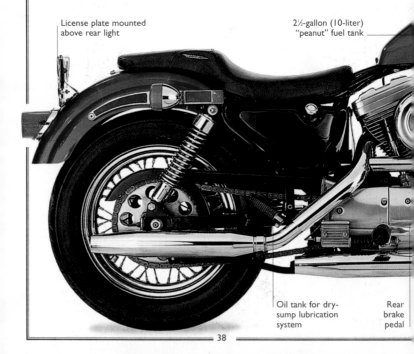

License plate mounted above rear light

2½-gallon (10-liter) "peanut" fuel tank

Oil tank for dry-sump lubrication system

Rear brake pedal

Traditional "Sportster" handlebars

SPECIFICATIONS

- **ENGINE** Overhead-valve, V-twin
- **CAPACITY** 54cu. in. (883cc)
- **POWER OUTPUT** 49bhp @ 7,000rpm
- **TRANSMISSION** Five-speed, chain drive
- **WEIGHT** 470lb (213kg)
- **TOP SPEED** 105mph (169km/h)

Speedometer

Air filter

Headlight peak

Fork yoke

Mudguard

FRONT VIEW

Alloy rocker cover

SIDE VIEW

Both wheels had a single 11½-in (29-cm) disc brake

1988 FLHS ELECTRA GLIDE

• THE EPITOME OF HARLEY-DAVIDSON •

HARLEY-DAVIDSON'S MOST FAMOUS MODEL was introduced in 1965, when an electric starter was added to the Duo Glide model to create the Electra Glide. The model received only minor updates until 1984, when the heavily revised "Evolution" engine was fitted. Performance figures and price have never been an issue with the Electra Glide. Comfort, long-distance ability, and the badge on the tank are all that matter.

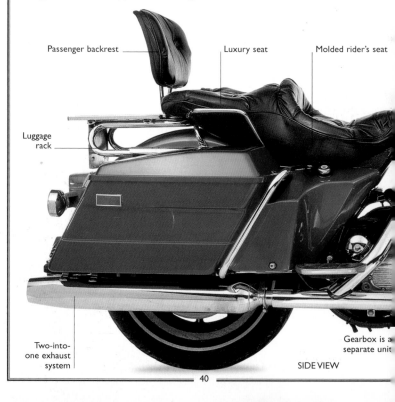

Passenger backrest

Luxury seat

Molded rider's seat

Luggage rack

Two-into-one exhaust system

Gearbox is a separate unit

SIDE VIEW

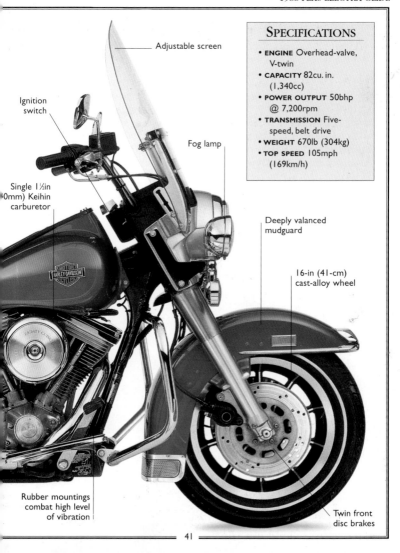

Adjustable screen

Ignition switch

Fog lamp

Single 1½in (40mm) Keihin carburetor

SPECIFICATIONS

- **ENGINE** Overhead-valve, V-twin
- **CAPACITY** 82cu. in. (1,340cc)
- **POWER OUTPUT** 50bhp @ 7,200rpm
- **TRANSMISSION** Five-speed, belt drive
- **WEIGHT** 670lb (304kg)
- **TOP SPEED** 105mph (169km/h)

Deeply valanced mudguard

16-in (41-cm) cast-alloy wheel

Rubber mountings combat high level of vibration

Twin front disc brakes

1997 FLHR ROAD KING

• A STYLISH RETURN TO TRADITION •

BY THE 1990S, HARLEY-DAVIDSON was a remarkable success story with a unique model range. Using its 1340cc engine in one of four chassis and equipped with a variety of cycle parts, Harley could claim a complete range of large-capacity machines for every type of customer. The Road King was a return to the original Electra Glide concept. It had the traditional Harley-Davidson attributes of comfort and relaxed long-distance ability, combined with the improvements resulting from continual development. No one could deny the importance of its classic looks. For most owners, buying the bike is just the start; it provides a base to which they can add a plethora of extras.

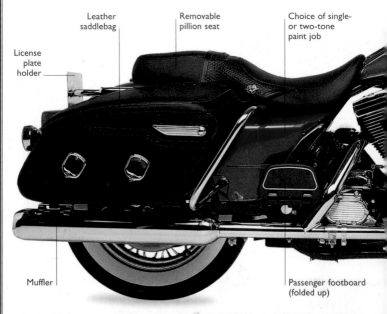

Leather saddlebag

Removable pillion seat

Choice of single- or two-tone paint job

License plate holder

Muffler

Passenger footboard (folded up)

Detachable
windshield

SPECIFICATIONS

- **ENGINE** Overhead-valve,
  V-twin
- **CAPACITY** 1340cc
- **POWER OUTPUT** 69bhp
- **TRANSMISSION** Five-speed,
  belt drive
- **WEIGHT** 692lb (314kg)
- **TOP SPEED** 96mph
  (155km/h)

Brake
pedal

Passing light

Traditional
valanced
mudguard

FRONT
VIEW

Chrome
trim

Whitewall
tire

Air filter

Wire-spoked
wheel

SIDE VIEW

43

INDEX

ACKNOWLEDGMENTS

AUTHOR'S ACKNOWLEDGMENTS:
Special thanks to John Lewis, Jeremy Pick, Roy
Pinto, and Roger Atyeo at Harley-Davidson UK,
Jim Rogers, and everyone who allowed us to
photograph their motorcycles. This book is
dedicated to Roger and Jenny. Good luck.

**DORLING KINDERSLEY WOULD LIKE TO THANK
THE FOLLOWING FOR THEIR ASSISTANCE:**
Frank Degenero; Deutsches Zweirad Museum
NSU Museum, Neckarsulm, Germany; Motorcycle
Heritage Foundation, Westerville, Ohio; The
National Motor Museum, Beaulieu, UK; The
National Motorcycle Museum, Birmingham, UK;
Jeremy Pick; and Dick and Wanda Winger.

**DORLING KINDERSLEY WOULD LIKE TO THANK
THE FOLLOWING FOR THEIR KIND PERMISSION
TO USE THEIR PHOTOGRAPHS:**
Harley-Davidson Motor Company Archives:
17 top left, 23 bottom right.

All photography by Dave King and Andy Crawford.

NOTE
Every effort has been made to trace the copyright
holders. Dorling Kindersley apologizes for any
unintentional omissions and would be pleased,
in such cases, to add an acknowledgment in future
editions.

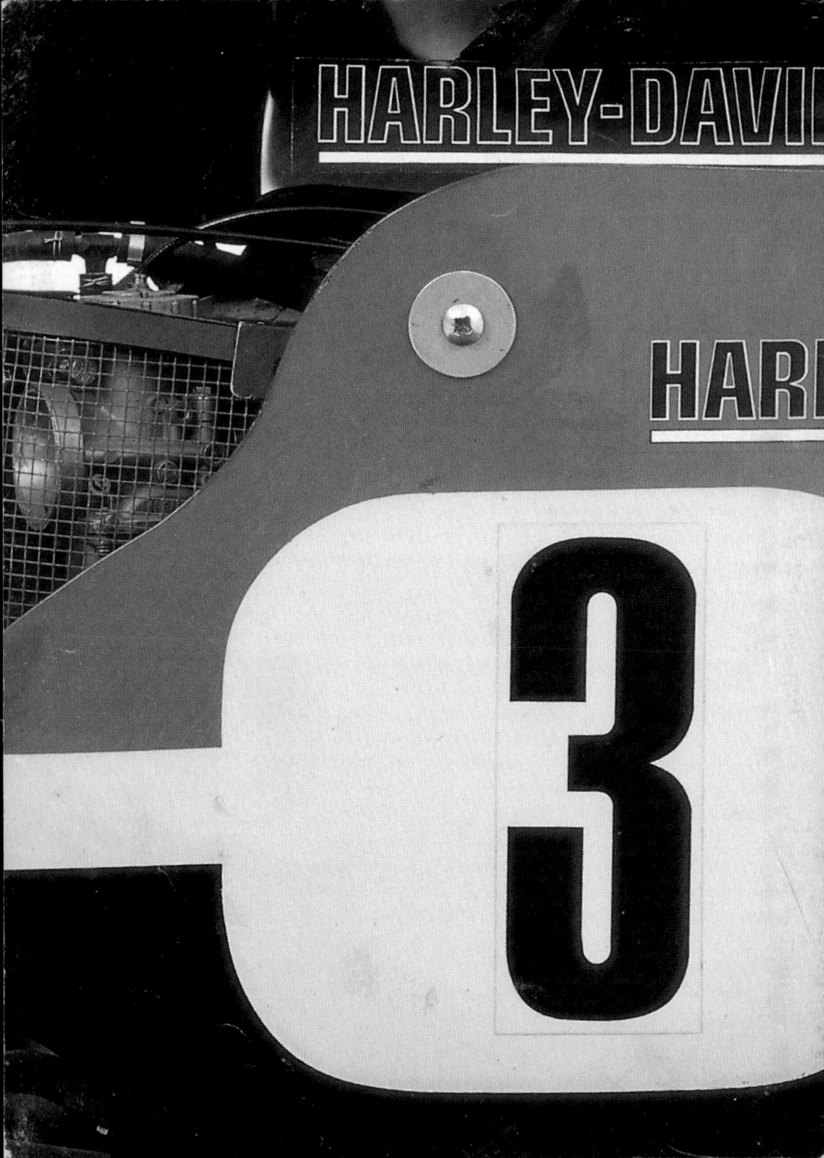
HARLEY-DAVI
HAR
3